THE HOW AND WHY WONDER BOOK OF

THE FIRST WORLD WAR

Written by Felix Sutton
Illustrated by Robert Doremus

Editorial Production:
Donald D. Wolf

Edited under the supervision of
   Dr. Paul E. Blackwood, Washington, D. C.
Text and illustrations approved by
   Oakes A. White, Brooklyn Children's Museum, Brooklyn, New York

WONDER BOOKS • NEW YORK

Introduction

Just 50 years ago, a gunshot rang out in a tiny town in troubled Europe and the First World War began. So the year 1964 marks an "anniversary" — but hardly the kind to celebrate happily. On the contrary, war — the very thought of war — is sobering. How else can we look back on the First World War and the march of events in that embattled period in man's history?

This *How and Why Wonder Book of the First World War* gives an authentic account of the day by day combat—in the trenches, in the sky, at sea—against its background of crises: how nation after nation aligned against other groups of nations; how the tide of battle turned again and again; how the hopes and fears of the people motivated their deeds; and, finally, how America helped to bring the war to an end.

To today's teen-agers, even the Second World War is distant and remote; the First World War seems like ancient history. Yet, neither of those wars is over the horizon of historic time. Someone in almost every family fought in one or both. The effects of both the First and Second World Wars have touched—even changed—the lives of each of us, young and old.

While you read this *How and Why Wonder Book of the First World War,* search for the clues that will help you understand better why nations engage others in war. Reading this book will strengthen the resolve of each of us to work in every possible way for a world of nations in which world, national, and individual goals can be realized without recourse to war.

Paul E. Blackwood

Dr. Blackwood is a professional employee in the U. S. Office of Education. This book was edited by him in his private capacity and no official support or endorsement by the Office of Education is intended or should be inferred.

Contents

Europe in 1914

What triggered the war?

The shot that triggered the War of 1914-1918 was fired by a 19-year-old student, Gavrilo Princip, in the little Balkan town of Sarajevo, capital of the Austro-Hungarian province of Bosnia, on June 28, 1914. Before its echoes died away, Europe was drenched in the most terrible blood bath the world had ever known; the war became known as "the First World War," because it was the first total war in history which involved whole nations, including civilians; it spread to 28 countries on six continents; battles raged on land from Africa to China, and on the seas from Jutland in the North Sea to the Falkland Islands in the South Atlantic Ocean; more than 10,000,000 men in uniform were dead, twice that many wounded, and more than 5,000,000 civilians killed, most of the European continent lay in ruins; the map of the world was changed; and "the war that was fought to end all wars" had set the stage for the Second World War 20 years later.

Bosnia had known a stormy past. Ruled by Croatian kings in the 10th century, occupied by Hungary in the beginning of the 13th century, it became an independent state during a short period of Serbian domination; conquered by the Turks in 1463, it became part of the Ottoman Empire. The scene of many insurrections against Turkish rule, especially during the beginning and middle of the 19th century, the powerful Austro-Hungarian Empire got a mandate after a bloody uprising in 1875 to occupy the country and keep the peace. In 1908, the Austro-Hungarian Government went beyond this mandate, annexed Bosnia formally, and made it a province of the Empire.

Many of the people of Bosnia, like Princip, were Serbian by ancestry and favored a union with other Slavic states free from Austro-Hungarian suppression, and now fought the Austro-Hun-

Gavrilo Princip kills Archduke Franz Ferdinand and his wife Sophie. Moments later, he was seized by officers, knocked down, and beaten nearly to death. He died in prison.

FRANCE

ENGLAND

RUSSIA

KING GEORGE V.

PRESIDENT RAYMOND POINCARE

CZAR NICHOLAS II.

TRIPLE ENTENTE (ALLIED POWERS)

ALLIED POWERS

CENTRAL POWERS

NEUTRAL POWERS

EUROPE, 1914

Before the echoes of Princip's shot had died away, mankind had plunged into the bloodiest battles it had ever known.

EMPEROR WILLIAM II.

GERMANY

EMPEROR FRANCIS JOSEPH

AUSTRIA-HUNGARY

TRIPLE ALLIANCE
(CENTRAL POWERS)

KING VICTOR EMMANUEL III.

ITALY

garian Government as they had fought the Turkish Government before. Many, like Princip, were members of the secret "Black Hand," a society of patriotic terrorists whose motto was "Union or Death." They thought they saw a chance for freedom when the Austrian Archduke Franz Ferdinand, heir to the throne of Austria-Hungary, came to Sarajevo on an inspection trip. A bombing attempt had failed in the morning, but as the car carrying the Archduke moved down the street later that day, Princip stepped out of the crowd, whipped out a revolver, and fired two shots. One struck the Archduke and the other his wife, killing them both almost instantly.

Princip's rash act was not, of course, the fundamental cause of the war. But it sparked the "dynamite" which had been piling up underneath Europe's placid surface for more than two generations.

What were the basic causes of the war?

Ever since the defeat of Napoleon a century before, England had been the richest and most powerful nation on earth. Her merchant marine and navy ruled the seas, and her army policed a colonial empire that girdled the globe. "The sun," Englishmen liked to boast, "never sets on the Union Jack." With raw materials from her colonies supplying her factories at home, England easily dominated world industry and trade. The pound sterling was the standard monetary unit in international finance. In virtually every aspect of world affairs, England was "top dog" — and she saw no good reason why things shouldn't stay that way.

On the continent of Europe, the leading nation was a young, vigorous, and upcoming Germany. She had won that position in 1871 after she had soundly whipped France in the Franco-Prussian War. Along with other spoils of that war, Germany had seized the province of Alsace and most of Lorraine, areas rich in mineral, farming, and industrial products. Soon, German products began to compete with those of England in most world markets.

To feed her booming factories, Germany needed more and more raw materials — and she soon acquired colonies in Africa and the Caroline, Marshall, Pelew, and Mariana Islands in the Pacific. This meant that she needed more merchant ships, and also warships to protect them. Kaiser Wilhelm II, Emperor of Germany, an arrogant, egotistical, ambitious young man, ordered his admirals to build a navy that was bigger than England's.

France itched for an opportunity to take revenge and to regain her position on the European continent. Britain peered fearfully over her shoulder at Germany's growing stature in world affairs. And so these two countries, France and England, adversaries since the days of William the Conqueror, suddenly found themselves in the unfamiliar position of allies with a common cause.

Meanwhile, the big Austro-Hungarian Empire was covetously eyeing the Balkan countries, and looking beyond them to the rich lands of the Near East. But Russia stood in their path. Russia, the largest country in the world, was also thinking about expansion — not especially in terms of more territory, but primarily to open up a passageway through the Straits of Bosporus and the Dardanelles into the Mediterranean for her merchant ships from the Black Sea. But the guns of Turkish forts blocked the way in these narrow waters. Even though its army, though huge, was the most primitive in Europe, and its navy a shambles, Russia, too, was spoiling for a fight.

In 1879, Germany and Austria-Hungary had signed a treaty which pledged each of these nations to come to the aid of the other in case of enemy attack. When, three years later, Italy joined the pact, this lineup became known as the Triple Alliance. By 1914, a similar mutual assistance agreement, the *Triple Entente,* existed between Great Britain, France, and Russia.

Thus the stage was set when the charge from Princip's pistol blew up the powder keg. The major European powers had already chosen their places on the stage.

Blaming the Archduke's assassination on Serbia, contending that Princip and his five fellow conspirators had received their guns and bombs in the Serbian capital of Belgrade with the knowledge and help of Serbian officials, Austria sent a stiff ultimatum to Serbia. It looked to a "police action," a localized war that would not only satisfy its urge for Balkan conquest but also serve as an opportunity to teach the Pan-Slavic movement a lesson and prevent other such anti-Austrian uprisings in other parts of the monarchy with predominant Slavic population. Germany encouraged Austria, being convinced that the powers of the *Triple Entente* would not interfere. Russia, fearing more Austro-Hungarian expansion and feeling compelled to do so as the major power of the Slavic nations, let it be known that it would stand on Serbia's side under any circumstances. Frantic diplomatic negotiations started, Germany and Austria still convinced that even if Russia would enter a war, France and England could be persuaded to stay out of it. None of the nations directly or indirectly involved, however, would risk the loss of face, would risk giving the impression of being too weak to fight or to live up to the commitments. Serbia would not bow to the Austro-Hungarian ultimatum.

Austria, refusing international arbitration, declared war on Serbia July 28, 1914. Russia ordered a general mobilization. So did Germany and France. In those days, mobilization meant war. On August 1, Germany declared war on Russia, and on August 3, on France. Great Britain declared war on Germany on August 4, after the German Army had invaded Belgium, whose neutrality had been guaranteed by England. The "localized war" Austria and Germany had hoped for had become within a few days a war between two powers of the Triple Alliance, the so-called Central Powers, Austria and Germany; and those of the *Triple Entente,* England, France, and Russia with the two small countries of Serbia and Belgium on their side.

(Italy, the third member of the Triple Alliance, deserted its allies, making the legal excuse that the obligation of mutual assistance existed only if one of the partners was attacked, but that under the circumstances, she didn't have to join her allies; they had declared war on the others.)

The Central Powers were joined on October 30, 1914, by Turkey and on October 5, 1915, by Bulgaria. The three powers of the *Triple Entente,* which became known as "the Allies" were joined by 22 nations, both great and small, before the war was over.

NEWSPAPER HEADLINES, AUGUST, 1914

Badly prepared and equipped, the tiny Belgian Army nevertheless tried to hold back the German onslaught. Dogs were used to make up for the lack of mechanized weapons; they pulled machine guns and carriages laden with ammunition.

The War in the West to 1917

THE GERMAN ATTACK

A German plan for the quick conquest of France, the so-called Schlieffen plan, had been worked out to the smallest detail by the head of the German General Staff, General von Schlieffen, 10 years before and then filed away in a top-secret drawer until the time was ripe. On the day Germany declared war, a huge German army of more than a million men moved swiftly to put it into action.

What was "the Scrap of Paper"?

The plan called for four German Army units to pour through Belgium and thence down in a great scythe-like sweep through France. The primary objectives were twofold: (1) to capture Paris, and (2) to squeeze the life out of the French Army in the grip of a giant pincers. The fact that tiny Belgium was neutral — and that, moreover, its territorial integrity had been assured by Germany as well as by England and France many years before — made no difference to the German war lords. When this treaty was brought to the attention of German Chancellor von Bethmann-Hollweg, he shrugged it off as being "just a scrap of paper."

When the war broke out, General Helmuth von Moltke, who had taken over as Chief of Staff of the German Army, changed the stoutly-designed Schlieffen Plan, which had envisioned an invasion through Holland and Belgium to avoid the French border fortresses. At the same time, a German army stationed in Lorraine was supposed to withdraw slowly in case the French would attack there and lure the French deeper into the trap between the big sweep of the main forces, with which the retreating army from Lorraine would finally unite for the last fatal blow. Moltke attacked

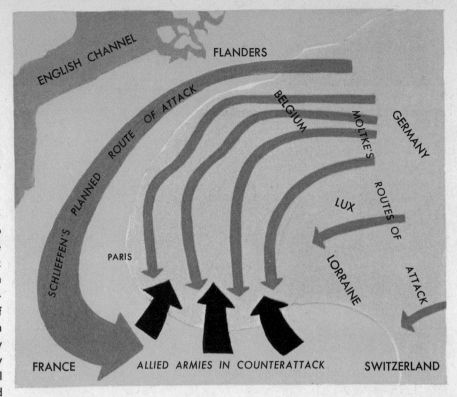

only through Belgium and Luxembourg. When the French, instead of concentrating on defense, attacked the Germans in Alsace-Lorraine as predicted by Schlieffen, Moltke did not order a slow retreat of his army, but instead withdrew troops from the right wing, weakening it heavily, and tried to hold the French advance in Lorraine by launching a counteroffensive. While the Schlieffen Plan had called for a sweep around Paris, Moltke shortened the right wing east of Paris, allowing the French and British troops to make a stand at the Marne that finally stopped the German offensive.

KING ALBERT OF BELGIUM

The Belgian population, trying to flee from the Germans, often got in the way of their own soldiers and disrupted their orderly retreat.

The German General Staff calculated that they could polish off France before the bumbling Russian Army could even organize. Then, they would turn east and take care of the Russian Bear. The more confident estimates in Berlin were that the war would be finished in six weeks. Some of the more conservative generals suggested two months as more "realistic" timing.

German intelligence did not expect Belgium to resist. But the little Belgian Army, hastily put into the field by King Albert, fought courageously in defense of their homeland. In a matter of days, however, despite the help of French troops, their forts and their defensive trenches were pounded to a pulp by the heavy German siege guns. Brussels and Liège fell to the invaders. The population scattered throughout the countryside, trying to flee from the Germans; but they only succeeded in clogging all the roads, making any orderly retreat of their own soldiers impossible. They also got in the way of advancing units of the German Army.

In spite of the fact that King Albert's army was weak and badly equipped — some of their antiquated machine guns were pulled by the big shaggy dogs that normally pull milk carts through the streets of Belgian towns — their fierce fighting spirit held up the German advance long enough to throw the Kaiser's timetable out of kilter.

But even though it was slightly behind schedule, the grim German steamroller swept onward into France. The French tried valiantly to stop them, but they were no match for the Kaiser's men, who had been training for this campaign for 10 years. A small British force landed in France and quickly jumped into the scrap. But they, too, went down like ripe wheat before the relentless German scythe.

Despite the miscalculation that the Belgian Army would not fight, despite a communication breakdown caused by the destruction of French telegraph lines, the German Army stormed across two-thirds of France just one month after it had crossed the Belgian border, and reached the Marne River, only 15 miles from Paris. On its banks, French resistance stiffened. The French commander, General Joffre — his troops affectionately called him "Papa" — vowed the Germans would never go beyond this point.

Meanwhile, King Albert and what was left of his battered army fought their way into the northeast corner of Belgium, the famed Flanders, and dug in.

THE BATTLE OF THE MARNE

In the lines along the Marne, 2,000,000 men were locked in deadly combat — a million on each side. The French and English were

What was "the Taxicab Army"?

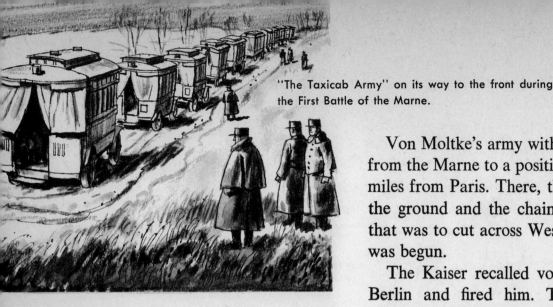
"The Taxicab Army" on its way to the front during the First Battle of the Marne.

desperate. If they lost Paris and if they had to retreat toward the English Channel coast, they would soon be in the hands of the enemy. The Germans, on the other hand, were frustrated. The conquest of France was not going according to their well-laid plans.

At one point in the fighting, it looked as though the French line would give way. Hurriedly, the French commander put in a call to Paris for more troops.

During the night, all of the taxicabs and buses in the city were rounded up to rush these 6,000 reinforcements to the Marne. Hundreds of vehicles streamed out from Paris. It is doubtful that "the Taxicab Army" turned the tide of battle. But it has come down in history as one of the great moments of World War I.

What really happened was that German General-in-Chief von Moltke panicked and changed the German master plan. In trying to pull the various parts of his far-flung "scythe" movement together, he actually opened up gaps between them which the combined French and British forces could attack piecemeal. When he lost contact with some of his commanders, a general German retreat was ordered in the confusion.

Von Moltke's army withdrew slowly from the Marne to a position nearly 50 miles from Paris. There, they dug into the ground and the chain of trenches that was to cut across Western Europe was begun.

The Kaiser recalled von Moltke to Berlin and fired him. The German grand plan for a quick and easy victory had gone up in the battle smoke along the Marne.

When the German armies were finally stopped at the Marne, the High Command devised a new plan. They proposed to strike northward to the English Channel ports of Calais, Dunkirk, and Boulogne, bring the southern coasts of England within range of their high-powered cannon, and cut off the British line of supplies.

What was "the Race to the Sea"?

In Belgium, British Tommies held the northern part of the Allied line as far as the town of Ypres. Beyond Ypres to Nieuwpoort on the North Sea, it was manned largely by what Belgian Army King Albert had salvaged after the fall of most of his country to the invaders. Fighting with the British were regiments of Sikhs, Ghurkas, and Rajputs from the British armies in India.

The Germans struck Nieuwpoort, Ypres, La Bassee, and Arras, the four main points of the Allied defense, almost simultaneously in late October. They were about to take Nieuwpoort when the Belgians opened the dykes of

In the first few months of the war, British cavalry, using lances, courageously but vainly charged German artillery units and machine gun nests. The toll they paid for their bravery was heavy.

Left to right: a French, a German and a British, infantryman in full battle dress. (The French red trousers, visible for miles, were changed later for blue.)

They didn't have enough reserve forces to combat the combined strength of French, British, and reinforcements from Canada (who were, incidentally, seeing their first European action). Stiffened Allied resistance pushed them back, too, at both La Bassee and Arras.

The battle at Ypres was the last big battle on the Western Front in 1914. It raged furiously from October 20 to November 11, with one side gaining a bit of hard-won ground only to lose it to the other. But at last, the German attack was beaten back. Both armies settled down in their trenches, where they would remain deadlocked, for the next two years. When the fighting stopped for a blessed hour or two, communiqués read: "All quiet on the Western Front."

the canals and flooded the battlefield. With much of their artillery lost in the deluge and thousands of their men drowned, the Germans were forced to backtrack. At Ypres, they failed, too.

THE TRENCHES

Trench warfare was not new — but only once before in the history of war had two stalemated armies settled down opposite each other in permanent trenches for such a prolonged siege of nerves. That was at Petersburg, Virginia, in 1864 and '65, during the American War Between the States. But the trench warfare along the Western Front in World War I made the Petersburg campaign look like child's play. World War I veterans recall it as devastating horror, saying that the only way a man could survive it was to learn to "see things but not feel them."

What was No Man's Land?

By the winter of 1914, a system of opposing trenches snaked some 600 miles down through the middle of France from the English Channel to the Swiss border. They were hastily dug at first as emergency defensive measures. But as the weary months dragged on, they were elaborated into extremely complicated systems. Second-, third-, and fourth-line trenches were constructed behind the first line, so that the troops could retreat from one to the other in case of overwhelming attack. All of these lines were connected by communicating trenches. Supply trenches were dug from the front lines as much as three or four miles back, so that replacement troops and supplies could be brought up from the rear without exposure to enemy snipers.

Officers' headquarters and first aid stations were located in dugouts. Hot

The battle at Ypres was one of the war's last trenchless battles.

food was brought up from field kitchens in the rear areas. The soldiers who manned the trenches — some in their early teens, others with only three weeks' training — stood around miserably in the mud, fighting off the rats and vermin that swarmed all over them at night.

At all times, snipers manned the "firing step" from which they could look across to the enemy trench and pick off anything that moved. When a number of them were shot through the head, crude periscopes through which the men could scan No Man's Land without exposing themselves to enemy fire were devised.

At some places, the trenches were but a mile or two apart; at others, they were as close as 30 or 40 yards. It was this, the intervening yards of torn-up, shell-pocked ground that was known as No Man's Land simply because no man could venture into it with much hope of coming back alive. On both sides, No Man's Land was bounded by the thick barricades of barbed wire that protected the front-line trenches.

Even so, patrols ventured out into No Man's Land nearly every night to try and find out what the enemy was up to. But before long, both sides began sending up flares which lit the night sky to high noon brightness, and such patroling became even more risky. Actually, the patrols made very little sense, for both great armies were hopelessly bogged down.

At the crack of dawn, the heavy artillery from behind the lines began lobbing shells into the opposing trenches. And the bombardment usually kept up,

off and on, all day. Soldiers just huddled deeper in their dugouts when the shelling started; hundreds of men were killed every day.

Every day or so, after the artillery bombardment at dawn, the men in the front lines would be ordered "Over the top!" in a charge that was meant to take the enemy trench by storm and capture it. But most of these charges, doomed to failure before they started, ran up against solid walls of machine gun bullets. On the rare occasions they succeeded, the trenches were usually quickly retrieved by men from the second and third lines of defense.

The longer the futile slaughter of trench warfare went on, the more impregnable the trench systems became. The commanders of both armies began to realize that the war was going to be a murderous stand-off unless one side thought of some sort of "secret weapon." Both the Germans and the Allies desperately set out to find one.

The Germans found theirs first. One morning in the spring of 1915, when the dreary warfare in the trenches had dragged itself out for more than six blood-soaked months, Allied

What was the Germans' "secret weapon"?

soldiers at Ypres saw a yellowish-green mist move slowly toward them. It was chlorine gas! Behind the windswept clouds marched a line of German infantry.

The deadly gas finally reached the soldiers. Choking, blinded, vomiting, they ran in panic. Terrified of their own poison, the Germans advanced cautiously; now and then, vagrant puffs of wind would blow the gas back into their faces. The breaches made in the Allied line were but momentary; reserves quickly plugged up the gaps.

Gas masks were issued to all front-line personnel for protection from the gas attacks made off and on throughout the war. But horrible as it was, poison gas did not prove to be the breakthrough the Kaiser and his generals had hoped for.

Trench warfare on the Western Front went on and on. No one — on either side — could see an end to it.

SLAUGHTER AT VERDUN

It was the beginning of 1916 and the Western Front was still in the grip of a bloody deadlock. The glorious German dream of winning the war in six weeks had

Who said, "They shall not pass"?

faded in the grisly reality of No Man's Land. Still, they held Belgium and all of the industrial areas of France. A dozen efficient railroads stretched back into Germany to provide an endless supply line. The German High Command now decided that the time had come for an all-out thrust in the West, one tremendous sledge hammer blow that would end the war.

As their striking point, they chose the fortress city of Verdun, the pride of France. The battle that followed lasted for 10 months — from February to December, 1916 — and has gone down in history books as one of the bloodiest ever fought. In the slaughterhouse of Verdun, more than half a million Frenchmen were killed, wounded, or captured. The Germans had promised, "There won't be anything left living out there. . . ." Their casualties, however, were nearly as great.

The Germans opened the melee with a 12-hour artillery barrage during which more than a million shells pounded the

A look into one of the trenches, for so long "home" for so many — friend and foe alike.

"Over the top" was the command that began the daily charges and that cost so many lives without changing anything.

15

German mine-throwers bombarded Allied trenches with deadly explosives continuously.

The tank, the British secret weapon during the battle at the Somme in 1916, was not too successful at first.

The flame-throwers first used by the Germans during the Battle of Verdun frightened even the German troops.

•

By 1918, the tank, armed with cannons and machine guns, was a formidable weapon. Here are 1918 models of French "land battleships" in action.

French. On the heels of the barrage came wave after wave of infantry. Yet, even in the face of this powerful steamroller, the French defenses held firm.

At the height of the battle, an unknown *poilu* (as the French privates were called) shouted: "Ils ne passeront pas!" And this "They shall not pass!" became the inspired French battle cry until the siege had at last ended.

The fighting raged with hardly a letup all through the spring, summer, and fall. It will never be known how many tens of millions of heavy artillery shells the Germans showered down on the enemy trenches, and the French big guns thundered back. The area between the opposing armies became a churned-up wasteland, spattered with shellholes, littered with the pieces of blown-up trees — and men. French soldiers said it was as if the enemy had pointed one cannon at each of them. Crazed by the horror, many men mutinied and others shot themselves. At one place, an entire trench was filled up by the debris of an explosion; only the tips of the soldiers' bayonets protruded above the ground. (After the battle, the French left it as it was, a memorial to their brave dead.)

The Germans lobbed shells into the French trenches that were filled with a new and even deadlier kind of poison gas, so that the defenders had to wear gas masks around the clock. Gradually, the whole city was reduced to formless rubble.

Verdun was surrounded by a string of forts; some of these fell to the Germans after furious fighting. Later, they were recaptured in counterattacks just as fierce. About midway through the battle, some of the French leaders suggested that the army should fall back and surrender the city to the attackers. At this, French General Joffre declared that any officer who ordered a retreat would be court-martialed and shot.

Despite the power of their attack, despite their superior numbers, despite their excellent supply lines and the inadequate ones of the French, the Germans could make no headway against Verdun. By December 15, they abandoned their plan and withdrew.

If it can be said that any good came from the tragedy of Verdun, it was the fact that the heroic resistance of their men strengthened the resolve of the people of France to win — if only in the name of their dead.

THE BLOODY SOMME

While the fighting at Verdun was at its peak, the British mounted a massive attack

What was England's "secret weapon"?

against the German lines along the River Somme, a little more than a hundred miles to the north. Unfortunately, they elected to hit what was probably the Germans' strongest defenses on the entire Western Front.

General Sir Douglas Haig, the British commander, lined up 1,500 big guns along an 18-mile front, placing them about 20 yards apart. On July 1, 1916, this mighty battery opened up, spewing out a mass barrage of death and destruction, possibly the heaviest of the war. Thus began a bloody battle that raged back and forth for four months.

In many respects, the Somme was like

17

Verdun. Although more than a million men died in the futile attacks and counterattacks, neither side accomplished anything of real importance. But each side bled the other white.

It was at the Somme that the British unveiled their "secret weapon." They intended it to be the key to the deadlock of trench warfare. And, indeed, it did much to change fighting tactics. The new weapon was the tank.

Brain child of British Col. Ernest D. Swinton, the tank was a heavily armored adaptation of the Holt Caterpillar farm tractor that had been developed in Peoria, Illinois. Manned by crews of eight, they carried either six-pound guns or machine guns, and rumbled along the terrain at a pace of four or five miles an hour. Officially, the machines were known as "land battleships." But for the sake of secrecy, the crates in which

they were shipped to the front were labeled "Tank." This is the name that stuck.

When the tanks first made their appearance at the Somme, British soldiers were just as surprised as the Germans; and the Germans were terrified. The tank could move across trenches and crush machine gun nests on its way, thus opening a hole for the infantry to attack through. The first clumsy tanks bogged down after a while in the battlefield mud. But new and improved versions were later developed by both the British and Americans.

The casualties at the Somme were even more ghastly than those of Verdun. The British lost 420,000; the French, 195,000; and the Germans, 650,000.

The British did not achieve the breakthrough that Haig had hoped for. They did, however, recapture about 200 square miles of territory and push the German lines farther back. The Western Front settled back once again to the grim business of a war deadlocked in the trenches.

1917 — "THE FATEFUL YEAR"

The year 1917 began as a bad one for the Allies. The Germans were solidly entrenched behind what they called the Hindenburg Line, a defensive zone that was 20 miles wide in places.

Why was General Nivelle replaced?

At Easter, the British and Canadians

In July, 1917 — when what was officially called "the Third Battle of Ypres" and popularly referred to as "the Battle of Passchendaele Ridge" began — not much was left of the city of Ypres.

attacked Arras where the Line's northwestern flank was anchored on Vimy Ridge. They made a little progress, but at a terrible cost in casualties.

All spring, the British had been digging a long tunnel under the Line at Messines Ridge. In May, they loaded it with a million pounds of dynamite and set it off. The ridge and the German trenches on top of it were blown skyward, and the British swarmed through. In the end, however, this advance was stopped, also.

In April the French, too, mounted a grand assault on the 50-mile German front from Soissons to Rheims. They were defeated so badly that the troops went on strike. General Nivelle, who had planned the ill-fated attack, was replaced by General Henri Pétain, the hero of Verdun. He put down the mutiny and restored some semblance of *esprit de corps* to the discouraged troops.

At Passchendaele Ridge, in July, and again at Cambrai, in November, the British tried twice more to breach the formidable Hindenburg Line. Although Canadian troops succeeded in taking the Ridge and tanks, now perfected, were first used in mass (a formidable 324) at Cambrai, quick German counterattacks won back a large part of the Allies' gains.

The Eastern Front to 1917

At the beginning of the war, the Russians were full of fight. Their army, known as "the steam roller,"

What was the Russians' great weakness?

and the largest the world had ever known, numbered 15,000,000 men. On paper, this looked like a force vast enough to mow down any opposition it came up against. But the figures gave a false picture.

Russia, country of illiterate peasant farmers, lacked the industry necessary to win a modern war. Consequently, they rushed to war deficient in artillery, airplanes, trucks, and motor cars. They didn't even have enough shells for the few big guns they possessed. The individual soldiers were armed, at best, with outmoded rifles. The Russian cavalry, the dreaded Cossacks, had a fearsome reputation. But as tactical military units, they were next to worthless. Moreover, the officers, selected usually for social reasons, were poorly trained; most of the non-coms, the corporals and sergeants who are the backbone of any infantry, could not even read or write. Radio communication and field telephones were all but unknown to the Russian forces.

Worst of all, Russia had virtually no railroads over which troops could be moved and supplied. Stacked up against

the crack German armies, the dynamic German industrial complex, and the super-efficient German transportation system, the stumbling Russian war machine was licked before it started. But the Russians didn't know it. Almost as soon as war was declared, the Czar's army moved on East Prussia, determined to take the fortress city of Königsberg, close to the German-Russian border on the Baltic Sea.

Southeast of Königsberg, they encountered a natural defense, the 50-mile long Masurian Lakes. Accordingly, the Czar split up his army into two separate forces, one to attack north of the Lakes and the other to make a swing south of them. The southern army was commanded by General Alexei Samsonov; the northern, by General Pavel Rennenkampf.

Now, such was the sorry organization of the Russian armies that the two commanders had been bitter enemies since their youthful days. They did not speak to each other personally, and once they were in the field, they refused to communicate with each other.

The German commander in East Prussia, General Max von Prittwitz, with not many more than 195,000 men at his disposal, had received the difficult assignment from the German Chief of the General Staff von Moltke of defending East Prussia and halting the Russian armies until Germany was victorious in the West and could switch the armies from the Western Front to the East. But he could not afford to risk his army. He was torn between the desire to attack and the urge to retreat.

Rennenkampf crossed the German border with his 200,000 men or so on August 17, 1914. He succeeded in defeating the German troops in his path and started his triumphant march on Königsberg. General von Prittwitz suggested to Berlin to order a retreat, even if it meant the sacrifice of East Prussia. Instead, the German Supreme Command recalled von Prittwitz and turned command of the armies in the East over to General Paul von Hindenburg, whom they had recalled from retirement, and made General Erich von Ludendorff, who had won praise during the Battle of Liége on the Western Front, his Chief of Staff. Together with Lieutenant

Sabers drawn, a unit of the dreaded Cossacks charges.

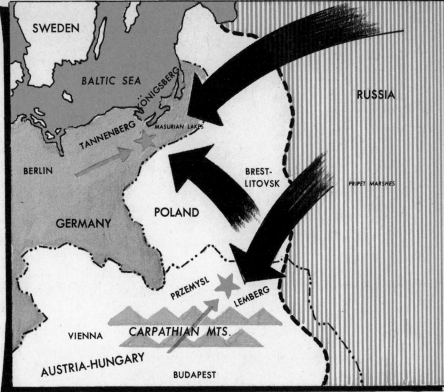

The map gives the location of the major events on the Eastern Front.

Colonel Max von Hoffmann, one of von Prittwitz's staff officers, they made an excellent team which fully exploited the sorry situation within the Russian command. Von Hindenburg took over command on August 23 and was master of the situation just a few weeks later.

At Tannenberg, south of the Lakes, von Hindenburg pounced on Samsonov's army and — in the last week of August, 1914 — destroyed it. He then loaded his troops in railway cars, took them north of the Masurians, and gave the same bitter medicine to Rennenkampf one month later. In a matter of days, the Russian armies were reduced to a shambles. They retreated pell-mell back into Mother Russia, and there they began to dig defensive trenches.

The Russians had better luck when they met the enemy along the Austrian border. In Galicia, their sheer numbers sent the Austrian armies reeling back-

ward in defeat, and they penetrated deep into the Carpathian Mountains after taking the Austrian fortresses of Lemberg and Przemysl. The Austrian armies collapsed, but they were saved from utter disgrace by German reinforcements. Now the German Kaiser knew that the storied military might of the Austro-Hungarian Empire was going to be of no use to him. If Germany was to win the war, she would have to do it by herself.

The temporary Russian victories in Galicia were as devastating to the Russians as they were to the Austrians. The men ran out of food, guns, and ammunition. Pressed by the Germans, they slowly stumbled backward into that part of Russia which is now Poland. There, like their brothers up north, they dug trenches. And the war in the East settled down to the same frustrating stalemate as in the West.

Offstage in Africa and the Pacific

On August 23, 1914, only three weeks after the fighting started in Europe, Japan declared war against Germany. But the crafty Japanese had no intention of sending troops to help the Allies in France. The principal war aims of Emperor Yoshihito and his war lords were territorial booty and prestige. Japan's social and political sun had been rising since the Russo-Japanese War. Japan's true motives, however, would not reveal themselves until a quarter-century later; at the time, they were not considered.

Why did Japan declare war?

Germany had established a colony at Kiao-Chau in the province of Shantung on the Chinese coast. Here, they had built a strong naval base for their Pacific fleet. Now, with the help of British naval squadrons, the Japanese attacked the German stronghold. After a three-month campaign, the German garrison surrendered. Thus, Japan gained its first beachhead on the Chinese mainland of China.

At the same time, Japanese and British fleets attacked and captured the German-held Pacific islands. As a result, the strategic Marshalls, Ladrones, Pelews, and Carolines were later mandated to Japan by the victorious Allies. And so, Japan got the South Pacific bases that were to play such a vital part in her Pacific conquests of 1941-42 during the Second World War. By these swift moves, the Japanese adroitly took what they wanted out of the turmoil of the European war. Then, they settled back and watched the rest of it from the sidelines.

There were four German colonies in Africa — Togoland, the Cameroons, German East Africa, and German Southwest Africa. These were attacked at the war's beginning by

What happened to the German colonies in Africa?

French and English colonial troops. Sporadic fighting in the jungles and on the rivers and lakes went on for more than a year. The Germans could not spare troops from the European fronts for reinforcements. By the middle of 1916, Germany's African possessions were in Allied hands.

The bright German hopes of winning the war in a hurry were growing dimmer and dimmer.

Even though the fate of the German colonies was decided, one German officer still kept on fighting. Lieutenant Colonel (later General) Paul von Lettow-Vorbeck had been stationed in German East Africa when war broke out in 1914. For four years, he led the British a merry chase through its jungles. Even after German East Africa was cleared of regular German troops by the British, he and his band of guerillas remained uncaptured. They would appear out of the jungle, stage a sudden raid on a British outpost, and than vanish into the jungle again. He was the despair of the British, but in all that time they were never able to catch up with him.

On November 23, 1918, twelve days after Germany signed the Armistice, von Lettow-Vorbeck heard of it while leading his men on a raid through Northern Rhodesia. Still undefeated, he went in to a British headquarters and honorably surrendered.

Turkey, Italy, and the Balkans

GALLIPOLI

Since Russia had practically no such industry of her own, she was dependent upon England and France for guns, munitions, and sundry supplies with which to fight the war. The Russians would repay their allies with shiploads of wheat and other foodstuffs. But the only route between the Mediterranean and Russia's Black Sea lay through two narrow channels, the Dardanelles and the Bosporus, farther north. Both were dominated by Turkey.

When, in November of 1914, Turkey, who had signed a secret agree-

Why were the Dardanelles important?

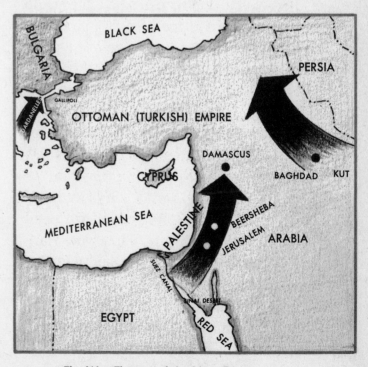

The War Theater of the Near East.

ment with Germany, came into the war on Germany's side, these two passage-ways were closed as tight as a corked bottle. For the Russians, this was disaster.

But young Winston Churchill, then First Lord of the British Admiralty, argued that the passages could be forced open by a direct frontal attack by battle-ships. He claimed that the operation would shorten the war by at least a year, perhaps two. Over the objections of some members of the British War Council, Churchill's plan, foolhardy as it was, was adopted.

In February of 1915, a British-French fleet of 16 major battleships, accompanied by mine sweepers and other auxiliary craft, steamed to the attack. In the narrow waters of the Dardanelles, they ran into a heavy field of mines, and a murderous cross fire from Turkish big guns in the forts along the shore. In the first attempt to force open the Strait, one French and two British battleships were sunk; the rest of the fleet, stopped cold, was compelled to withdraw from the hapless operation.

The British then decided to make a landing on the narrow Gallipoli penin-sula, which lies between the Dardanelles and the Aegean Sea. Not only was this one of the worst-planned expeditions in military history, but the Turks knew all about it through information gathered by their spies in Egypt. They were wait-ing with big guns and barbed wire en-tanglements when the first of the British forces began to land.

The result was a bloody slaughter. British and Anzac (Australian-New Zealand Army Corps) troops were mowed down by the tens of thousands as they tried to gain a toe hold on the beaches. Everything from the landing of supplies to care of the wounded was in a state of wild confusion. To make mat-ters worse, there was no water on the Gallipoli desert, and men began to die of thirst. But for all the odds against them, the invading troops managed to secure a tenuous beachhead along the shore; there, they dug in.

The bitter, fruitless fighting went on for six months until the British leaders in London realized that the whole thing had been a ghastly mistake from the be-ginning and ordered a withdrawal. Winston Churchill, who had planned the operation, was removed from his Cabinet post in disgrace.

The campaign for the Dardanelles and Gallipoli was one of the most tragic of the entire war. Fortunately for Brit-ain, Churchill profited by their lesson and survived disgrace to become one of "the Big Four" of World War II.

For the war in the Near East, both sides depended heavily on the "ship of the desert," the camel.

WAR IN THE NEAR EAST

In the fall of 1914, the British landed an expeditionary force of Indian soldiers in Mesopotamia, Turkish territory on the Persian Gulf, and quickly took the key city of Basra. Their objective was twofold: to protect British oil interests in that part of the Near East, and to weaken Turkey's war effort by encouraging the Arabs to revolt against their hated Turkish masters.

What was "the hell of Kut"?

Sadly underestimating his foe, the British general ordered an advance into the desert to capture Baghdad, of *Arabian Nights* fame. On the way, the army took the miserable little desert town of Kut al Imara, which was nothing more than a forlorn group of mud houses baking under the scorching desert sun. Seeing no sign of hostile Turks, the British moved on toward Bagdad.

Within sight of the ancient city, the army was suddenly jumped by a Turkish force about twice its size. After losing nearly half his men in the battle that followed, British General Townshend beat a retreat back to Kut.

There, a huge Turkish-Arab army surrounded the trapped British troops and settled down for a prolonged siege. With scant food and water, almost no medical supplies, and no hope of relief, the Britishers were holed up in Kut for nearly five months. Men died like flies from hunger and tropical diseases. Finally, the pitiful remnants of the army, about 9,000 "dirty skeletons in rags," surrendered to Field Marshal von der Goltz, supreme commander for the Central Powers in Mesopotamia.

Who was Lawrence of Arabia?

In the Syrian Desert, nearly a thousand miles west of ill-starred Kut, the British had better luck. After beating off an attack by Turkish troops on the Suez Canal, Lloyd George in London ordered the army to proceed into Palestine, which

25

was part of the Turkish Empire, and capture Jerusalem.

At first, it was tough going. The Turks were used to the desert and the British were not; in the first months of the campaign, British defeats were severe. Then, a new general, Sir Edmund Allenby, nicknamed "the Bull" because he was huge and forceful, came out from England to take command. British fortunes began to look up. One of Allenby's greatest pieces of luck was his meeting with a strange young man named Thomas E. Lawrence.

Lawrence was a little fellow, scarcely five feet tall, but his body seemed made of steel wire. He had been an archaeologist digging up desert ruins when the war started, and had become the leader of the Arab revolt against the Turks after being sent to Egypt to head the military intelligence there. His men called him "Wrecker of Engines," because he had been harassing the Turks by wrecking their railway trains by blowing up bridges and tearing up tracks. He was to become famous in the history books as Lawrence of Arabia and for his own account of his adventures, *The Seven Pillars of Wisdom*.

Allenby decided to work with the little fighting rooster, and gave him almost limitless access to guns and supplies. It was the wisest decision of the entire Near East campaign.

Although he held the rank of captain in the British Army, Lawrence always dressed in the long, flowing native desert costume complete with sword and disdained all military formality. His Arabs were a wild lot, and only "El-Aurens" could control them. But they made the life of the Turkish Army miserable, surprising them in groups and often killing them to the last man.

Meanwhile, Allenby built up a large army. Just before Christmas of 1917, with Lawrence raiding the Turks and cutting their railroads and supply lines, Allenby was able to take Jerusalem. A few months later, again with Lawrence's help, he defeated the Turks at the decisive battle of Megiddo. This battle, in which Allenby captured 76,000 prisoners, was a decisive factor in finally eliminating Turkey from the war. Turkey surrendered on October 30, 1918.

ITALY, RUMANIA, AND BULGARIA

Italy was in the Triple Alliance with Germany and Austria-Hungary, but had refused to go to war against Britain and France in 1914 on the grounds that Germany was the aggressor. As a result, both camps tried to woo her to their side. Germany promised expanded territory; the Allies, part of Austria and colonial possessions in Africa. The Allied offer looked most lucrative; so Italy came into the war on the Allied side on May 23, 1915.

Why did they declare war?

Italy was ill-prepared for war: Her army was far from up-to-date. Her scant heavy industry would never supply a war effort. Her people did not want to fight. When the Italians attacked Austria in the rugged Alpine country to the north, it had little effect. Nothing much was happening on the Italian front compared to the earth-shaking events in France. General Cadorna and his army had had to retreat when a strong German-Austrian army of about 400,000 men attacked the Italians in May, 1916, on the Isonzo River.

Then, on October 24, 1917, a huge army of Germans and Austrians suddenly struck at Caporetto, in northern Italy. The Italian line crumbled and the soldiers fled in panic behind the Piave River, where they made a stand with the help of the British and French. The disaster at Caporetto knocked the Italians out of the war as a national fighting force although Italian regiments continued to fight alongside the French and British on the Western Front.

Rumania, too, had been bargaining with both sides. Then, on August 27, 1916, she made up her mind to throw in with the Allies. Almost at once an Austrian-German army attacked the Rumanians; in three months, she was utterly defeated. Rumania's quick collapse provided Germany with much-needed oil from the rich Rumanian oil fields and thousands of tons of wheat from her rolling farmlands.

After having driven the Russians out of the Austrian lands which today comprise Poland, the German armies set out to finally punish Serbia. Belgrade, the Serbian capital, fell before the Germans and Austrians on October 9, 1915. Bulgaria, who hoped to recover territory lost in 1913 to Serbia, declared war on Serbia on October 11. The Serbian losses were terrible; and many Serbs fled to Albania and Greek islands.

Greece, torn between its King Constantine, who favored the Germans, and its pro-Allied Prime Minister Venizelos, for the other side, had tried to stay neutral but was finally forced into war on June 27, 1917, on the Allied side.

Specially trained and equipped Italian mountain troops prepare an attack in jagged Alpine territory.

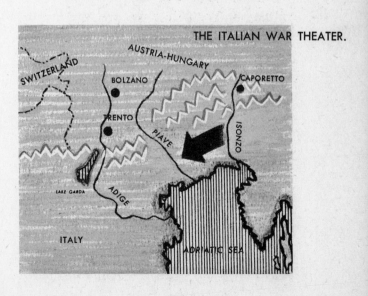

THE ITALIAN WAR THEATER.

SWITZERLAND

AUSTRIA-HUNGARY

BOLZANO

CAPORETTO

TRENTO

PIAVE

ISONZO

LAKE GARDA

ADIGE

ITALY

ADRIATIC SEA

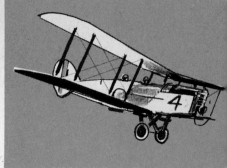

Some early Allied planes, from left to right: the Nieuport 17 (the favorite plane of the British ace, Albert Ball); the Breguet 14 bomber (a two-seater built in France); the British-built DH-9A bomber; the S.P.A.D. (a French-built fighter plane preferred by many American pilots).

War in the Sky

Who were "the Aces"?

The airplane was but in its infancy when World War I burst into flame in 1914. The Wright brothers had made their first faltering heavier-than-air flights — the longest of which had lasted less than a minute — only 11 years before. Yet, the airplane developed faster and further in the four years of the war than any other weapon in history in a comparable period of time.

In the beginning, flimsy biplanes, built like the original Wright pusher, flew over opposing lines to observe the movements of enemy troops. Sometimes, a British pilot would pass close to a German pilot. On these occasions, both fliers would wave a gallant salute to each other. High above the filthy mud and blood of the battlefield below, they felt that they were knights of the sky.

Then one day, one of these British "knights" got an idea. He put a pistol into the pocket of his flying suit. The next time a German plane flew within range, instead of saluting, he fired. After that, all the pilots on both sides carried hand guns, and the brief age of chivalry in the air was finished.

Within the next year, airplane design advanced tremendously. The Wright-type "Flier" gave way to a comparatively solidly-built ship with biplane wings and an engine mounted in front of the fuselage. A light machine gun, secured to the top wing, fired over the propeller. This was an awkward arrangement, however, for it was almost impossible for a pilot to aim his gun at an enemy plane.

Then, a young Dutchman named Anthony Fokker, who designed fighter planes for the Germans, began to ponder the problem. He later related that he got his great idea one night after he had gone to bed, jumped up, went to his drawing board, and had the whole design on paper by morning. The conception was simplicity itself — to an engineer. Let the motor fire the gun! And synchronize it, so that the bullets would pass through the propeller blades when the blades were out of the line of fire! Now, the German pilot could aim

"Dogfight" between German Albatross and British Martinsyde fighters.

his plane directly at an enemy craft and knock it down with precision.

For several months, this revolutionary gun gave the Germans a decided advantage in aerial warfare. Allied pilots were calling themselves "Fokker fodder." But it didn't take British and French engineers long to catch on to what Fokker had done. When they did, German and Allied fliers were fairly evenly matched. Their planes, highly maneuverable, could fly from 100 to 140 miles per hour. Most of the victories then went to the pilots with the greatest flying skill.

Although by 1917, both sides had developed large bombing planes that carried one or two men besides the pilot, aerial bombardment did not play too decisive a part in the battles of

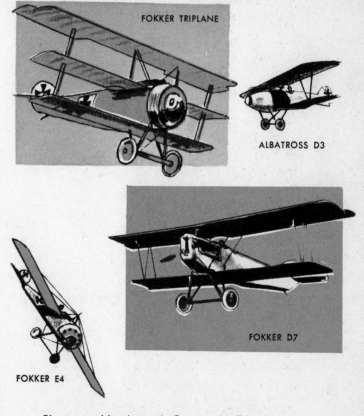

FOKKER TRIPLANE

ALBATROSS D3

FOKKER E4

FOKKER D7

Planes used by the early German Air Force.

World War I. Scouting and observation (reconnaissance) continued to be the prime function of the air forces.

A more glamorous use of the plane, however, in the war — and the one that made newspaper headlines — was the shooting down of enemy aircraft. Any pilot who destroyed five or more enemy planes was designated as an "ace."

The leading ace was a German, Baron Manfred von Richthofen, "the Red Knight," who had 80 single-handed kills to his credit before he in turn was shot down in flames by a kid from Canada named Roy Brown. Captain René Fonck was the top French ace with a score of 75. Captain Edward Mannock held the British record of 73.

Close on his heels was Canadian Major Billy Bishop with his 72. (In World War II, Bishop was Air Marshal of the Royal Canadian Air Force.)

The American "Ace of Aces" was Captain Eddie Rickenbacker, a former automobile test driver who had started out in the war as General Pershing's chauffeur. He scored 26 victories during the few months that United States fighting planes were active. After the war, Captain Rickenbacker organized, and is now president of, one of America's leading commercial airlines.

One of the most terrifying aircrafts —

What was a Zeppelin? to civilians, at least — developed during the war was the German Zeppelin. It had been invented several years before by a German scientist, Count Ferdinand Zeppelin, as a peace-

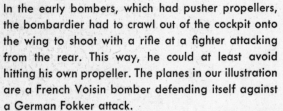

In the early bombers, which had pusher propellers, the bombardier had to crawl out of the cockpit onto the wing to shoot with a rifle at a fighter attacking from the rear. This way, he could at least avoid hitting his own propeller. The planes in our illustration are a French Voisin bomber defending itself against a German Fokker attack.

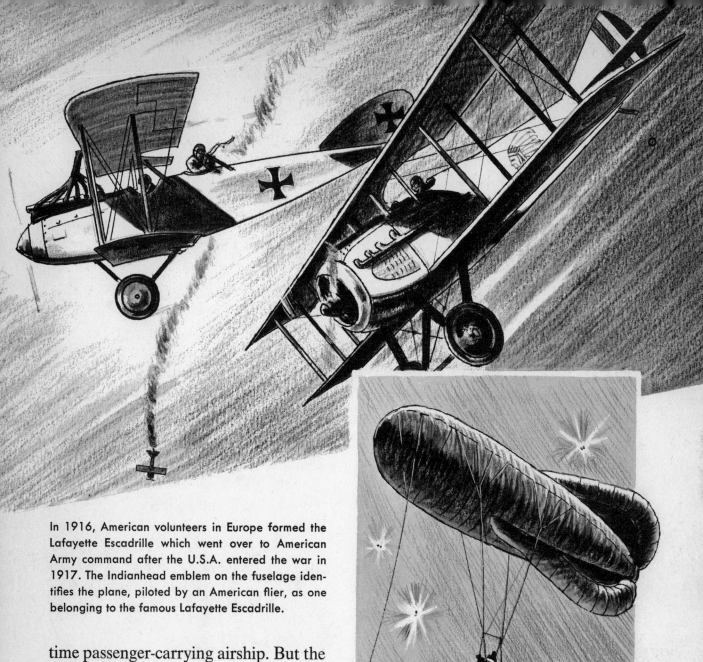

In 1916, American volunteers in Europe formed the Lafayette Escadrille which went over to American Army command after the U.S.A. entered the war in 1917. The Indianhead emblem on the fuselage identifies the plane, piloted by an American flier, as one belonging to the famous Lafayette Escadrille.

Both sides used lighter-than-air craft in the form of observation balloons. In the German "sausage balloon," the observer, in a wicker basket hanging from the balloon, kept a close eye on the front.

time passenger-carrying airship. But the Kaiser's High Command at once saw its possibilities for the bombing of English cities, specifically London.

"The Zep," as it was called, was a lighter-than-air craft, shaped like a huge cigar and nearly 700 feet long, about the length of two and a half football fields. Through the middle, it was 72 feet thick. Its framework was a light but strong aluminum alloy covered with airplane cloth. It was buoyed up, like a balloon, by hydrogen gas. Six engines propelled it through the air at a top speed of about 60 miles per hour. It carried an observation car that could be lowered by a thousand feet of steel cable. Thus, the Zeppelin was able to sail along above the clouds while the observer swung beneath them and reported his findings by phone.

Crew quarters were inside the hull;

crews on duty rode in twin gondolas slung underneath the ship. The Zeps were armed with machine guns and light cannons — and they carried 300 fire bombs!

But for all its formidable appearance, the Zep had a number of severe drawbacks. Hydrogen gas, for one thing, is highly inflammable. If the ship was hit by an incendiary bullet, or if any sort of stray spark was struck inside it, the entire craft exploded in a furious burst of flame. So, Zep crews really had the most dangerous jobs of the war. Moreover, being lighter than air and bulky, the Zep was almost impossible to control in a high wind.

The Germans hoped that their Zeppelin fleet, by burning the city of London and destroying English industry, might bring the English people to their knees. But, like poison gas, it was another "secret weapon" that failed. The Zeps did their bombing at night, and at first, the civilian population was terrified. But soon, they found that the German bombs did little real damage, and relatively few people were killed. After a number of raids, so many Zeps were shot down in flames that the Germans concluded that the results were not worth the cost. They called the bombing campaign off.

Actually, the Zeppelins had an effect the Germans never expected. The ruthless killing of innocent women and children and the demolishment of their homes infuriated the British people and stiffened their will to defeat the German "murderers." In the United States, people were horrified at such wanton brutality. America was brought a step closer to entering the war on the side of the Allies.

The Zeppelin, a huge lighter-than-air dirigible, did not fulfill the expectations of the German High Command.

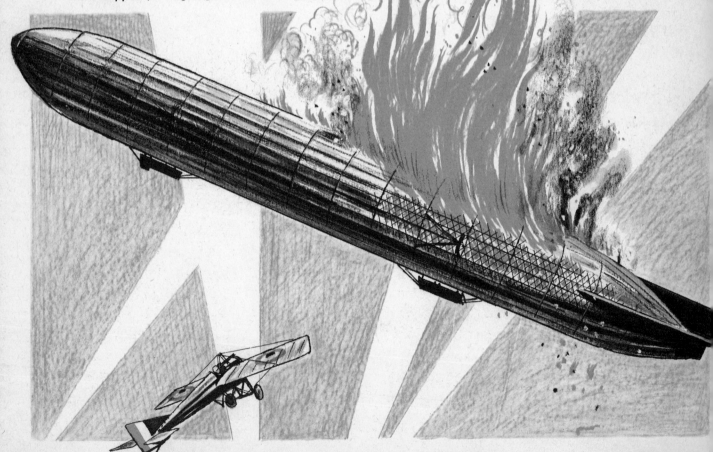

The War at Sea

What was the U-Boat campaign? Next to Britain, Germany had the most powerful navy in the world. But the German fleet was based at Kiel, in a bay of the Baltic Sea, and it was almost impossible for the battleships and cruisers to put to sea without being detected and engaged by the British. For the first two years of the war, the German fleet practically rusted at its moorings in its home harbor.

Meanwhile, British warships were able to rove the world's oceans almost at will and clear the seas of German ships, both merchant and naval. Within a few months after the war began, the British Navy had clamped down an effective blockade.

Early in the fighting, then, it became apparent that Germany would have to rely on her submarines for action on the high seas. They called their undersea boats "U-Boats." German shipyards desperately worked to build a large U-Boat fleet as rapidly as they could. This was another of their tries at a "secret weapon."

In the spring of 1915, Germany boldly announced to the world that U-Boats would sink any Allied ships that appeared within certain specified "war zones" without warning. All ships, even those from neutral countries carrying supplies to England, were considered enemies. All of the neutrals, including the United States, protested what they considered "uncivilized" warfare. But the Germans replied that their U-Boats would continue to prowl the

German U-boat on blockade duty stops a British supply ship. The Allied crew takes to the lifeboats.

seas until the stranglehold on them was broken. It is estimated that during the course of the war, more than 4,000 ships, neutral as well as Allied, were sent to the bottom by German subs. Like the Zeppelin raids, the unrestricted U-Boat campaign had an adverse effect for the Germans. Public opinion in the United States turned sharply against Germany.

The turning point in the U-Boat war came on May 7, 1915. A week before, the *Lusitania*, Britain's newest and fastest luxury liner, had sailed from New York for Liverpool. Aboard her were 197 Americans, including women and children. Only a few miles off the Irish coast, she was struck by a torpedo from a submerged U-Boat. The stricken *Lusitania* sank in a matter of minutes, taking some 1,200 of her passengers with her to the bottom. Among the dead

Deadly torpedoes being loaded aboard a U-boat.

were 115 of the 197 Americans. The Germans defended the sinking by claiming that the *Lusitania* had been carrying munitions.

The people of the United States were outraged; "Remember the *Lusitania*"

became a rallying cry for war. It was only a question of time until the U. S. would enter the war on the side of the Allies.

There was only one major naval battle **What was the Battle of Jutland?** during the entire course of the war between the German High Seas Fleet and the British Grand Fleet. It took place on May 31, 1916, in the North Sea off the Danish peninsula of Jutland.

On May 30, Admiral Scheer, Commander in Chief of the German fleet, sailed into the North Sea with virtually all his heavy battleships, escorted by cruisers and destroyers. His purpose

After America entered the war, merchant ships and troop transports, protected by warships, traveled in convoys through the U-boat blockade. First came destroyers; then, cruisers and torpedo boats (with observation balloons) followed by files of merchant ships, flanked by trawlers for protection against torpedoes. More torpedo boats formed a rear guard. Destroyers circled the convoy constantly to engage and sink enemy U-boats.

was to try to come to grips with the British Grand Fleet and destroy it. A fighting admiral, he saw no point in a huge navy that simply stayed in its harbor and saw no action.

What Admiral Scheer didn't know, however, was that the British had broken the secret German code and thus, were warned of his plans. The British Commander, Admiral Jellicoe, at once took the Grand Fleet to sea to hunt down the Germans.

The two fleets clashed the next day, May 31. The main action, obscured by great clouds of black powder smoke, lasted only about two hours. But by the time the furious fighting was over and the battle smoke had cleared away, the British had lost three battle cruisers, three armored cruisers, and eight destroyers. The German losses were one battleship, one battle cruiser, four light cruisers, and five destroyers. The British loss in lives was 6,097; the German, 2,545.

The Prince of Wales, who was slated to become King George VI of England, fought as a junior officer on one of the British battleships.

But for all its sound and smoke and fury, the great sea battle proved nothing. When it was over, the German High Seas Fleet went back to its base to remain there, doing nothing, for the rest of the war. And the British retained their old command of the seas.

A German U-boat blows up her prize after the crew has abandoned ship.

The Battle of Jutland

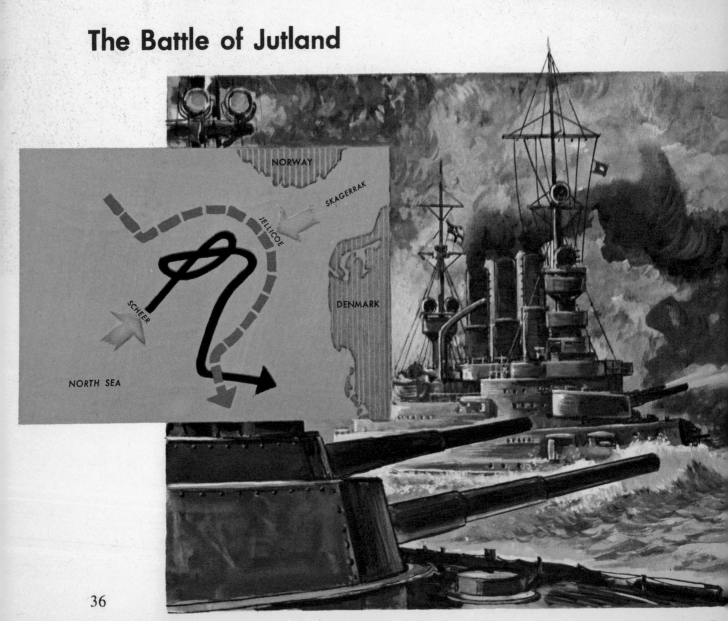

NORWAY

SKAGERRAK

JELLICOE

SCHEER

DENMARK

NORTH SEA

Close-up of the deck and turrets of the German battle cruiser *Seydlitz*, heavily damaged during the Battle of Jutland.

German battleships, all guns firing, engage British Dreadnoughts at Jutland.

The height of the Battle of Jutland: Scheer's battleships attack again.

The Course of the War 1917-1918

THE RUSSIAN REVOLUTION

Revolution had been brewing in Russia

Who was Rasputin? for a great many years before the war began. The Russian peasants owned no land of their own and lived in misery and want. The factory workers were little better than slaves, barely managing to eke out a meagre living from long hours of toil. The ruling classes were rich and all-powerful, and had no understanding or sympathy for the plight of the laboring masses.

Yet when war was declared, the Russian people responded with patriotic fervor, and rushed to the colors by the millions. But the eagerness of the common soldiers soon turned to gloom. Some of the men actually had no rifles. Food was scarce. Thousands went without shoes in the freezing Russian winters, and had to wrap their feet with rags.

Moreover, Russian casualties at the front were appalling. In one campaign — a futile effort to push the Austrians and Germans out of Poland in 1915 — the Russians lost more than a million men. The Russian soldier was just about ready to quit. All that was needed was a spark to light the fire. Ironically, it was set off in the palace of the Czar.

Since birth, the Czar's small son had been a victim of hemophilia, a rare blood disease which can cause its victim to bleed to death from even the smallest cut. The royal doctors could do nothing for it.

In 1905, a lay monk had appeared in Moscow to become known as a "holy

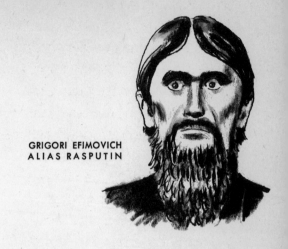

GRIGORI EFIMOVICH
ALIAS RASPUTIN

man," able to heal many ailments for which doctors knew no cure. His name was Grigori Efimovich, but he became known in history as Rasputin (really his nickname). He appeared a few years later in St. Petersburg as the leader of a new religious cult and was introduced at the court in 1907. He soon gained tremendous influence there in all matters, especially after the Czar and Czarina became convinced of his ability to cure their ailing son. When his political influence got in the way of some leading noblemen, the Czar was forced to banish him to Siberia in 1913, but he returned to St. Petersburg soon after the outbreak of the war to be received with renewed favour by the court. A sinister political influence, he coerced the Czar to hire and fire certain high officials, and his evil way of life lost for Czar Nicholas the little respect he had left.

Late in 1916, a group of noblemen succeeded in assassinating Rasputin, but the damage had been done by then. Revolutionary mobs stormed through all Russian cities crying for the end of the Czar's rule. Ordered to fire on the crowds, the soldiers refused and joined the Revolutionaries. A few months later, in March, 1917, the Czar was forced to abdicate his throne, and he and his family were imprisoned and executed not long afterwards.

The leader of the Revolution, Kerensky, formed a new Socialist government intent on carrying on the war on the side of the Allies. The Russian soldiers, however, had had enough of fighting. When a new offensive was ordered on the Galician front by General Brusilov, the soldiers refused to move, formed councils and elected their own leaders, left the ranks of the army, and started to walk home to get their share in the land of the rich promised them. Kerensky's government was overthrown by Lenin, the Communist leader, whom the Germans had helped smuggle into the country from exile in Switzerland.

Unable and unwilling to carry on the war, Lenin's government negotiated and signed on March 3, 1918, the peace treaty of Brest-Litovsk. The terms were harsh. The Russians had to give up most of their territory in eastern Europe, which meant half a million square miles of fertile wheatland and industry and 56,000,000 people. Most advantageous at the moment for the Germans, this separate treaty allowed them to release their troops from the Eastern Front for use in the West. For Britain and France, it was the war's lowest point.

Lenin addresses a meeting during the Russian Revolution.

Soldiers, sailors, and workers storm the Winter Palace in Petrograd, once St. Petersburg, on November 7, 1917. The Bolshevik Revolution under Lenin's leadership had begun.

February 2, 1917: President Wilson announcing to Congress the breaking-off of diplomatic relations with Germany prior to Congress' declaration of war on April 6, 1917.

UNCLE SAM DECLARES WAR

At the war's beginning, the people of the United States were determined to stay out of it, and to trade with both sides impartially. Most American sentiment was on the side of Britain and France, but there were also millions of Americans of German descent who sympathized with "the Fatherland." But on one thing, everybody agreed — it was Europe's private fight and none of our business.

Why did the Americans fight?

Little by little, however, Americans began to turn sharply against Germany. People were appalled at the ruthless invasion of neutral Belgium, the inhuman use of poison gas, the Zeppelin raids on London, the sinking of unarmed ships by U-Boats. When the *Lusitania* was torpedoed and innocent American lives were lost, this indignation reached a crescendo.

And the Germans did many other things that antagonized the American people. They sent spies into the United States to blow up munition factories as well as munition ships in the harbors. German agents, it was said, planned to poison drinking water in reservoirs in American cities.

Then, in February, 1917, the German Foreign Secretary, Alfred Zimmermann, made a very stupid move. He sent a note to the German ambassador in Mexico in which he proposed that if the United States entered the war against Germany, Mexico should immediately make war on the United States. Mexico's spoils of victory would be territory in Texas, New Mexico, and Arizona which had been lost to Mexico as a result of the Mexican War in 1848. The Zimmermann note was intercepted by the British and printed in American newspapers.

Ten days after this note was published, Germany announced a policy of completely unrestricted submarine war-

fare. Their U-Boats would sink any ship on sight regardless of the flag she flew, if the U-Boat commander had reason to believe that she was carrying goods to the Allies. This was the worst mistake the Germans could possibly have made. But by this time, they were so deeply involved that it was a case of "whole hog" or none at all. Besides, they were supremely confident of victory.

These two events, the Zimmermann note and the announcement of unrestricted submarine warfare — coming as they did only ten days apart — were the last straw. America made up her mind. On April 6, 1917, Congress declared war on Germany.

War fever ran high all over the country, but the United States was sadly unprepared to fight. Our Army was small and old-fashioned. Our Air Force was practically non-existent. Our Navy had been allowed to go to seed. America's first task was to build up an efficient fighting force.

"Preparedness" became a national crusade, and "The Yanks Are Coming" was heard all over the 48 states. Almost a million and a half men were selected in the first draft. Dozens of training camps were rapidly set up. General John J. ("Black Jack") Pershing, a seasoned veteran, was placed in supreme command.

With the Russian front collapsed, the French and British had their backs to the wall. They fervently prayed that the Americans would get to France in time.

And they did. A little more than a year later, early in the summer of 1918, a U.S. Army of 2,000,000 men, well-equipped and well-trained, landed in France and moved into the front lines. With their coming, the Germans were doomed.

THE YANKS GO INTO ACTION

In the spring of 1918, American troops,

What was "Big Bertha"?

a division at a time, began arriving in France to go into training camps there. But it would be

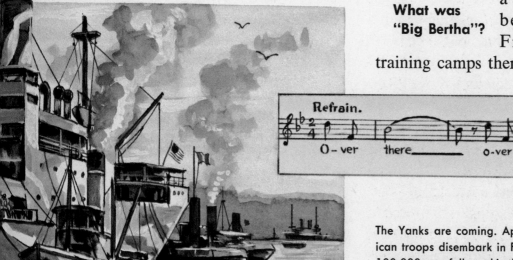

Refrain.

O-ver there___ o-ver there

George M. Cohan's "Over There" became the theme song of America's fighting men.

The Yanks are coming. April, 1918: The first American troops disembark in French harbors. More than 100,000 men followed in the first month alone. Wherever they showed up, they were greeted by the French population with wild cheers and flowers.

41

another two or three months before the A.E.F. (American Expeditionary Force) got to the front in large numbers. The French and British Armies were war-weary and discouraged by defeat. On the other hand, the Germans were being reinforced by troops released from the Russian front. Now, the German leaders thought, was the time for an all-out attack.

The German General Ludendorff began his attack on March 21 with a dramatic show of strength. For the first time, the Germans unveiled a giant cannon which they affectionately called "Big Bertha." Set up behind the Hindenburg Line, it could lob a shell into Paris, 75 miles away. At the top of its trajectory, the shell traveled 21 miles into the air. The world was flabbergasted at this stunning display of German science. The people of Paris were badly frightened. But for all her thunder, Big Bertha did very little real damage.

With the initial roar of the big gun, the German offensive struck. At the first fierce impact, it rolled back the British and French defenses. But after retreating foot by foot for 50 miles, the British line stiffened and held. The German advance was momentarily halted.

Then in May, Ludendorff moved forward again. This time, at the little village of Château-Thierry on the River Marne, the Germans ran into several A.E.F. Divisions that Pershing had rushed to the front. Like demons, the Yanks attacked and stopped them cold.

Not far from Château-Thierry was the German stronghold of Belleau Wood, a rough, forested area. A battalion of U.S. Marines was ordered to

capture it. Advancing into the face of overpowering machine gun fire, as well as clouds of poison gas, the brave Marines took the Wood. But they paid a terrible price for victory: more than half their number were killed or wounded.

The German advance was at last stopped, only 40 miles from Paris. And the Yanks had done it! German defeat was only a matter of time.

THE ALLIES ATTACK

The German Armies made one final desperate offensive drive in July. After a hard fight, American and French divisions, fighting shoulder to shoulder, turned them back at what is known as the Second Battle

What was "the Lost Battalion"?

The going was tough for the attacking American troops on the Meuse-Argonne front.

of the Marne. At long last, the German war machine—that had trampled so arrogantly across the Belgian border four years before — was on the defensive.

The stage was set for the Allied push that would end the war.

It would be a two-prong pincer attack, with a million Yanks under General Pershing pushing north through the Argonne Forest, east of Verdun; and an equally large army of British and French, under General Haig, breaking through in the Vimy-Arras sector. Other smaller Allied units, one of them led by Belgian King Albert, would strike the Hindenburg Line at points in between. French General Foch was the over-all commander.

The big push into the Argonne started on September 26. The forest was one of the most ancient wooded areas in France. Charlemagne had hunted stags and bears in its deep recesses more than a thousand years before. In 1917, it was still a tangled mass of thick woods covering a broken, hilly terrain. But the Germans had nearly every square foot of it fortified.

The Yanks found it tough going. Thousands of brave men died for every mile the A.E.F. advanced, and the field hospitals were filled to overflowing. But Pershing's men doggedly pressed on. It was in the heart of the gloomy Argonne Forest that one of the great adventures in American military history took place.

The 1st Battalion of the 77th Division ("New York's Own") had been assigned to go forward to take a certain ridge. As they moved through the wet,

43

silent woods, they could hear firing on both sides. Suddenly, without warning, they were surrounded by Germans. Quickly, the men dug a shallow circular trench and dropped inside. They began to return the fire from German rifles and machine guns that was pouring in on them from everywhere.

Major Charles W. Whittlesey, the commanding officer, sent messages for help by carrier pigeon. But it didn't come. The Yanks were running out of ammunition. Under a flag of truce, the Germans sent a message urging the men to surrender for humanity's sake. The Yanks refused. Airplanes tried to drop food and ammunition, but the packages, falling outside the armed circle, were seized by the Germans.

Amid the pounding of heavy artillery, mortar shells, machine guns, grenades, and rifle fire, the Lost Battalion managed somehow to hang on. On the fifth day, they were rescued. Seven hundred men went in with Major Whittlesey; less than 200 came out. The Lost Battalion became an American legend.

It was in the Argonne, too, that Alvin York, a farm boy from the hills of Tennessee, became one of the greatest heroes of the war. Leading a patrol through the thick woods, York accidentally got inside the enemy lines. When a machine gun opened up on the patrol, York quickly put it out of action with his rifle. (He had been the turkey-shooting champion back home.) Germans came out of the woods from all sides

The first contact between the German Army and American troops occurred in June, 1918. The advancing Germans had forced the French to retreat and give up Belleau Wood. The Germans stormed through the waist-high wheat (illustration at left) in hot pursuit of the French when they were stopped cold. The line of American Marines that had been quickly brought into action held. This was on June 3. On June 6, the 4th American Marine Brigade started the counter-offensive (illustration at right).

with their hands up. By the time he got back to his own lines, Alvin York was marching a veritable army of prisoners in front of his gun — 128 men and four officers!

Surrendering German soldiers are led away by their Allied captors.

THE ARMISTICE

A funeral service on the battlefield for one of the many American casualties.

By November 1, 1918, Pershing's men had fought their way through the Argonne to the other side. Now, they were advancing by leaps and bounds. To the north, Haig's British and French had shattered their part of the Hindenburg Line. The once-proud German Army was rapidly collapsing, and their fairly orderly retreat

What happened to the Kaiser?

turning into a rout. On September 29, 1918, Ludendorff declared that further resistance was impossible; he advised the German Government to ask for an armistice. The new German Chancellor, Prince Max von Baden, followed his advice and began armistice negotiations.

Back in Germany, the people on the home front were just as undone as the soldiers on the battle front. There was little or no food except potatoes and turnips. Germany had been fighting half a world virtually alone, and the dreadful casualty lists — practically every family had lost a father, son, or husband — had made the people sick to death of war. Even defeat was better than the life they had been living for over a year.

On November 10th, the Kaiser and his family fled to exile in Holland. And the next day, at 11 A.M., November 11, 1918, the last shot of the war was fired. A dead quiet settled over the Western Front. In a few weeks, birds began to sing again in the shattered trees.

Ironically, in Russia, Allied soldiers, including Americans, fought on for nine months after the Armistice was signed.

By November 4, all of Germany's allies, Austria-Hungary, Bulgaria, and Turkey had surrendered. Emperor Francis Joseph had died in 1916 to be followed to the throne of the Austro-Hungarian Monarchy by Charles IV. By the summer of 1918, the Hapsburg Monarchy was well on its way to dissolution. Uprisings were common in all the territories, and men were deserting the army on a large scale. Provisional Czech, Polish, and Yugoslav Governments were formed and legions of their soldiers were fighting on the side of the Allies. The armistice which was negotiated on November 3, 1918, marked the end of the Monarchy and the Empire. The Hungarian, Czech, Polish, and Yugoslavian provinces proclaimed their independence, and on November 13, the Republic of Austria was established.

The League of Nations

President Wilson called the war "a war to make the world safe for democracy." The people of the world took heart. Perhaps, this bloody holocaust had indeed been "the war to end all wars." In January of 1918, he announced America's plans

What were "the Fourteen Points"?

for permanent peace, which became famous as "the Fourteen Points." They outlined:

1. Abolition of secret treaties.
2. Freedom of the seas.
3. Removal of trade barriers between nations.

4. Reduction of arms.

5. Adjustment of colonial claims.

6. Restoration of Russian territory.

7. Restoration of Belgian territory.

8. Return of Alsace-Lorraine to France.

9. Readjustment of Italian frontiers.

10. Freedom for the people of Austria-Hungary.

11. Freedom for the Balkans.

12. Freedom for the people conquered by Turkey.

13. Establishment of an independent Poland.

14. Creation of a League of Nations.

Wilson dreamed of a war-free world. He did not wish to punish Germany for starting the war. But Prime Minister Lloyd George of England and Premier Georges Clemenceau of France, had different ideas. Their countries had been badly hurt by German aggression, and they wanted revenge.

At the Peace Conference at Versailles on June 28, 1919, — just five years to the day after Gavrilo Princip fired his fatal shot—the leaders of England and France, over Wilson's protests, imposed harsh and humiliating punishment on Germany in the way of loss of territory and reparations.

Ironically, the United States was the only major nation that refused to join the League. The American people were tired of war, and fed up with Europe's problems. They wanted to get back to "good old American normalcy."

The League of Nations faltered along from its beginning, and just before the outbreak of World War II, it died. But out of Woodrow Wilson's great dream grew the idea of our present United Nations, depended on by people the world over to keep the peace.

What Did the War Cost—in Lives and Money?

The worst loss that nations suffer in war is in loss of lives.

It is estimated that the death toll among soldiers in World War I rose to 12,991,000.

To this frightful figure must be added an estimated 10,000,000 civilian dead from famine, disease, and privation caused by the war.

In addition, more than 21,219,000 soldiers were wounded, many of these men incapacitated for life.

In dollars and cents, the cost of the war has been reliably fixed at $337,-980,579,657. (This figure includes military supplies, shipping losses, property damage, and losses in production.) We are still paying the bill.

What a terrible price the whole world has had to pay for the ambitions of a handful of men greedy for power and prestige.

HIGHLIGHTS OF THE FIGHTING OF WORLD WAR I

1914

Aug. 4 German Army invades Belgium.

Aug. 7 Russian Army invades East Prussia.

Aug. 20 Germans occupy Brussels. First German air raid on Paris.

Aug. 22 Germans invade France.

Aug. 23 Japanese forces attack German colony at Kai-chau.

Aug. 26-31 Russians defeated at Battle of Tannenberg.

Aug. 28 British cruisers raid German naval base at Heligoland; are driven off.

Sept. 1 French Army defeated at Soissons; begins retreat through France.

Sept. 3 French Government moves from Paris to Bordeaux.

Sept. 6 Battle of the Marne begins.

Sept. 6-15 Russians defeated at Battle of Masurian Lakes.

Sept. 10 French repel Germans at Marne.

Sept. 12 Beginning of trench warfare.

Oct. 5 Germans advance on Warsaw.

Oct. 25 Attack on Warsaw fails.

Nov. 7 Kai-chau surrenders to Japanese. (At about this same time, Japanese forces occupied the German Pacific Islands: Marshalls, Mariannas, Carolines, Palaw.)

Nov. 17 Germans repulsed at Ypres.

Dec. 14-24 British attack on Nieuport; Verdun line bogs down.

Dec. 24-25 British Air Force raids German positions in Belgium.

1915

Jan. 8 Germans make slight gains against Allied lines at Soissons.

Jan. 31 Germans renew attack on Warsaw.

Feb. 12 Germans invade Russia.

Feb. 19 Allied naval squadrons bombard Dardenelles; are repulsed.

Feb. 26 Heavy fighting at Champagne; the battle is a stand-off.

Mar. 20 Zeppelin raids on Paris.

Apr. 22 Second Battle of Ypres; Germans introduce poisonous gas.

Apr. 25 British and ANZAC troops land at Gallipoli.

May 1 Turks attack British beachheads at Gallipoli.

May 7 *Lusitania* sunk by German U-boat.

May 9-June 18 Second Battle of Champagne; no gain for either side.

May 23 Austrians attack Italian forces.

May 25 Winston Churchill resigns as First Lord of British Admiralty.

May 26-31 Zep raids on London.

June 21-July 1 Heavy fighting at Gallipoli.

July 1 Heavy fighting in Argonne sector.

July 15 Conquest of German South Africa completed.

Aug. 5 Germans take Warsaw.

Aug. 12-Sept. 8 Severe Zeppelin raids on London.

Sept. 23 Big Allied offensive opens on Western Front.

Oct. 2 Worst Zeppelin raids to date on London.

Oct. 13 English nurse Edith Cavell shot as spy by Germans.

Dec. 7 Seige of Kut-al-Imara by Turks.

Dec. 8 British begin retreat from Gallipoli.

1916

Jan. 19 Gallipoli evacuated by British and ANZAC forces.

Jan. 29-31 Zeppelin raids on Paris and London.

Feb. 2 Heavy fighting between Austrians and Russians.

Feb. 21 German attack on Verdun begins.

Mar. 25 British destroyers and planes raid Zeppelin hangers at Schleswig.

March 30 British hospital ship sunk by Turks in Black Sea.

Apr. 10 Germans gain at Verdun.

Apr. 29 British surrender at Kut.

May 15 Heavy fighting at Vimy Ridge.

May 31-June 1 Battle of Jutland.

June 5 Austrians advance in Italy.

June 16 Germans advance to within four miles of Verdun.

July 1 Battle of Somme begins; first use of British tanks.

Sept. 12 French advance on the Somme.

Oct. 7 German submarine U-53 reaches Newport, R.I.

Oct. 8 U-53 torpedoes five ships off Nantucket.

Oct. 22 Russians defeated in Galicia.

Nov. 18 Battle of Somme ends.

Nov. 21 Emperor Franz Joseph of Austria-Hungary dies.

Nov. 28 First German airplane raid on London.

Dec. 10 German commercial submarine, *Deutschland,* completes second voyage to United States.

Dec. 15 French drive Germans back, win victory at Verdun.

1917

Jan. 8 German High Command decides on unrestricted submarine warfare.

Jan. 19 Von Zimmerman note to Mexican Ambassador urging a Mexican alliance with Germany against the U.S.

Jan. 31 Germany notifies U.S. that unrestricted U-boat warfare will begin Feb. 1.

Feb. 3 U.S. severs relations with Germany.

March 8 Russian Revolution begins.

March 11 Baghdad occupied by British forces.

March 15 Czarist Government overthrown in Russia.

April 3 Germans retreat to Hindenberg Line after massive British and French attacks.

April 6 U.S. declares war on Germany.

Apr. 9 Battle of Arras begins; British take Vimy Ridge.

Apr. 16-20 Second Battle of Aisne; British and French suffer heavy losses.

June First U.S. troops land in France; General Pershing commanding.

June 7 British launch mass surprise attack on Messines Ridge.

June 31-Nov. 10 Third Battle of Ypres; British troops gain about five miles at a cost of 400,000 men.

July Lawrence of Arabia emerges as legendary hero of the war in the desert.

Aug. 20-Dec. 15 Second Battle of Verdun.

Oct. 24 Italian line shattered by German-Austrian forces at Caporetto; Italians retreat in confusion.

Nov. 8 Bolsheviks overthrow revolutionary Russian Government under Kerensky.

Nov. 20-Dec. 3 Battle of Cambrai; British attack with 380 tanks; unable to follow their advantage.

Dec. 5 British withdraw from Cambrai.

Dec. 8 British conquer German East Africa.

Dec. 9 General Allenby takes Jerusalem.

1918

Jan. 6 Armistice between Germany and Russia.

Jan. 7 German sailors mutiny at Kiel.

Jan. 10 Russian Black Sea fleet mutinies.

Mar. 3 Peace treaty of Brest-Litovsk between Russia and Central Powers.

Mar. 21 German spring offensive begins on Western Front; British forces driven back at Ypres and Amiens.

Apr. 5 British and Japanese Marines land at Vladivostok.

Apr. 11 Germans take Armentières.

Apr. 22 British Navy raids Zeebrugge and Ostend.

May 7 Peace treaty between Germany and Rumania.

May 29 Germans take Soissons.

June 1 German offensive reaches Château-Thierry.

June 4 U.S. divisions help drive Germans back across the Marne.

June 11 Allied counteroffensive stops German advance.

July 10 French at Marne.

July 19 American cruiser, *San Diego,* sunk off Fire Island, N. Y.

July 21 Americans and French take Château-Thierry.

Aug. 7 German sailors mutiny at Wilhelmshaven.

Aug. 30 Germans retreat in Flanders.

Sept. 1 British advance in Macedonia.

Sept. 3 Germans retreat to the Somme.

Sept. 22 Allenby advances in Palestine.

Sept. 26 Americans and French launch Argonne attack.

Sept. 27 American Army provides vital strength that breaks the Hindenberg Line.

Sept. 29 Bulgaria surrenders.

Oct. 6 Americans take St. Étienne and La Château. First peace note sent by German Government to President Wilson.

Oct. 9 Allies retake Cambrai.

Oct. 12 Germans send second peace note to U.S. President.

Oct. 14 President Wilson replies; says peace terms must be left to military leaders, Germans must change their Government.

Oct. 17 Allies retake Ostend, Bruges, and Lille.

Oct. 30 Turkey surrenders.

Nov. 4 Austria surrenders.

Nov. 7 Americans take Sedan; break backbone of German resistance.

Nov. 10 Emperor Wilhelm flees to Holland.

Nov. 11 Germany signs armistice; firing ceases at 11 A.M.

Nov. 21 German Navy surrenders to British.

Nov. 25 Last remnants of German forces in East Africa surrender.

Dec. 6 American occupation troops enter Germany.

1919

Jan. 10 Austria signs peace treaty at Paris.

June 28 Germans sign Treaty of Versailles.